D1064049

Learning to Share My Faith

Chuck Kelley

LifeWay Press
Nashville, Tennessee

ISBN 0-8054-9864-8

This book is a revision of the Equipping Center module *Learning to Share My Faith* © Copyright 1990 of the Sunday School Board of the Southern Baptist Convention.

This book is a resource in the Evangelism category of the Christian Growth Study Plan
Course CG-0077

Dewey Decimal Classification: 248.5
Subject Heading: WITNESSING

To order additional copies of this resource: WRITE LifeWay Church Resources Customer Service; One LifeWay Plaza; Nashville, TN 37234-0113; FAX order to (615) 251-5933; PHONE (800) 458-2772; EMAIL to *customerservice@lifeway.com;* ORDER ONLINE at *www.lifeway.com;* or VISIT the LifeWay Christian Store serving you.

Printed in the United States of America

Leadership and Adult Publishing
LifeWay Church Resources
One LifeWay Plaza
Nashville, TN 37234-0175

Contents

1 Preparing to Lead Lost Persons to Christ

John and Susan were driving home after hearing a sermon on evangelism. "Do you ever feel guilty after the pastor preaches about witnessing?" asked John. "Not really," said Susan. "I know that witnessing is important, but I also know that I wouldn't be very good at it. Working with the children's choir is what I do for the church. I leave the witnessing to someone with more skills than I have. Each of us has a job, and no one has to feel guilty."

Have you had a conversation like that? Most Christians believe that evangelism is important. The real question, however, is the importance of evangelism for you. Is it necessary for you to be a personal witness to the saving power of Jesus Christ? Can you do something else for Christ and for the church while others witness?

Accept Responsibility for Witnessing

The apostle Paul expressed his feelings about being a personal witness in an unusual way. In Romans 1:13-15 he wrote of his desire to go to Rome as a witness for Christ. He felt that he owed the people of Rome a debt, and that debt was to tell them about Jesus. We are not surprised that Paul felt like that, but should we feel like that as well? Are we also obligated to tell others about Jesus?

Following are four reasons you need to witness.

Your neighbor. The people of the United States probably have greater access to the gospel than any other people in history. In spite of that, many have not heard it at all. Many more have not understood it. Here are some of the most common misunderstandings.

- You get salvation the old-fashioned way—you earn it. Do more good than bad, and you will be all right.
- All religions are the same. The important thing is to believe in a higher power.
- God loves us so much that He could never let anyone go to hell.

People with ideas such as these do not know the message of Jesus. From Romans 10:17 we learn, "Faith comes from hearing the message, and the message is heard through the word of Christ." Your neighbor needs to hear the gospel in order to believe.

This need is especially important in light of the consequences of unbelief. Read John 3:18,36. What is the result of a lack of faith in Christ? What are some of the present consequences of life without Christ? The person without a saving faith in Jesus is missing abundant and eternal life. All unbelievers will face God's wrath and judgment one day. The needs of our neighbors obligate believers to be personal witnesses.

Think of the names of two persons you know who have not been born again. If they became Christians today, how would their lives be affected?

_____

_____

How would their families be affected?

_____

_____

Are the potential changes worth the effort it would take to share the gospel with them? ❏ Yes ❏ No

Yourself. Talking about Jesus is also something Christians need to do for themselves. Personal witnessing is necessary for the spiritual health of the believer. Dialogue about your faith makes your spiritual life stimulating and meaningful. The more you talk to others about Jesus, the more excited you will become about your own faith and relationship with God. Talking to others about Jesus is a natural part of a Christian's life. If you spend time with God each day, you will naturally witness of your relationship with Him. Furthermore, as you grow in that relationship, others will come to you with questions or for help because your life resembles that of Jesus. Because you are growing in Christlikeness, you genuinely care about people. Therefore, you do not mind taking risks to witness to those you meet, even if you are initially uncomfortable doing so.

Personal witnessing is also a trigger that releases power in our lives. Read 1 Corinthians 2:1-5. In a surprising statement Paul admitted feeling weak and inadequate as he considered the task of bearing witness to Christ in the city of Corinth (see 2:3). As he spoke about Jesus, however, God demonstrated the presence and power of the Holy Spirit (see 2:4). Believers who witness about Christ experience the Holy Spirit working in and through their lives. God always gives power and strength to those who do His work.

Many Christians feel intimidated when they think about telling someone about Jesus. Yet those moments of weakness can be times when God provides His greatest strength. When Paul complained about the weakness he felt from a thorn in the flesh, the Lord taught him an important lesson: " 'My power is made perfect in weakness' " (2 Cor. 12:9). Christians who want to experience God's power will find it replacing their weakness as they share Jesus with others.

Your church. Personal witnessing is also a necessity for the life and ministry of your church. Baptisms in most mainline denominations have declined over the past several decades. How is your church doing in winning the lost?

The best way your church can increase the power of its influence in your community is to increase the number of witnesses who share Christ with others. The greatest power a church has is the willingness of its people to tell their friends and family members what Jesus has done for them. If churches multiply the number of people doing the work of evangelism, they can grow by adding new believers to the membership. Personal witnessing is a necessity for churches to grow through evangelism.

Your Lord. Although God does not need us to accomplish the salvation of lost people, He chose to involve us in the process. In His wisdom the Lord chose to use human agents to spread the news about new life in Jesus. God's plan for evangelism obligates Christians to be witnesses.

Among the last words of Jesus in each of the Gospels was a command for His followers to be witnesses of what they had seen and experienced. In Matthew He told the disciples to " 'make disciples of all nations' " (Matt. 28:19). In Mark they were commanded to " 'preach the good news to all creation' " (Mark 16:15). Luke records Jesus reminding the disciples that " 'repentance and forgiveness of sins will be preached in his name to all nations, beginning at Jerusalem' " (Luke 24:47). After the resurrection narrative in John, Jesus said: " 'Peace be with you! As the Father has sent me, I am sending you' " (John 20:21). Clearly, Jesus expected His followers to be witnesses for Him in the world.

Throughout the New Testament Christ's followers are admonished to speak about Jesus in the world. In 2 Corinthians 5:20 the apostle Paul noted: "We are therefore Christ's ambassadors, as though God were making his appeal through us. We implore you on Christ's behalf: Be reconciled to God." The dictionary defines *ambassador* as *an official messenger with a special mission*. Christians are official representatives of Jesus. Our special mission is to urge others to be reconciled with God through faith in Jesus.

Jesus referred to His disciples as fishers. In Matthew 4:19 He said, " 'Come, follow me, . . . and I will make you fishers of men.' " Jesus expected those who followed Him to become personal witnesses. Neither one's type of personality nor one's amount of Bible knowledge makes one a "fisher of men." We become witnesses as a result of what Jesus does for us. Since He chooses us to share, He will do what is necessary to enable us to witness. We must be involved in evangelism, for that is the work Jesus intends for us to do.

Do you think that God will judge Christians for their failure to tell others about salvation? ❑ Yes ❑ No

Read Ezekiel 3:16-19. What do you think these verses mean?

_____
_____
_____

Summarize why it is important for you to witness.

_____
_____
_____
_____
_____
_____

Begin to Pray

Jesus revealed the next step of preparation in Matthew 9:36-38. When He saw multitudes of people suffering distress and despair, He was moved with compassion. He realized that the number of workers did not match the size of the ready harvest. Instead of sending the few workers available immediately into the field to reap as much of the harvest as possible, Jesus told His disciples to "pray ye therefore the Lord of the harvest, that he will send forth labourers into his harvest" (Matt. 9:38, KJV).

Witnessing involves prayer. The disciples looked at the multitude and saw a large group of people. Jesus looked at the crowd and saw broken lives (see Matt. 9:36). His vision of their needs stirred His compassion. When our compassion is stirred, we will want to witness.

As we pray, God opens our eyes to see the harvest as He sees it. He gives us His vision, and that vision will compel us to share Jesus. Persons who pray for the harvest will want to work in the field, just as the disciples who prayed for laborers in Matthew 9 went out to share in Matthew 10.

Prayer also reminds us of the One to whom the harvest belongs. We are to ask the Lord to "send forth labourers into his harvest" (Matt. 9:38, KJV). The harvest is from the Lord, not from the laborer. As laborers we are instrumental in bringing persons to Christ, but God is responsible for their salvation (see 1 Cor. 3:6).

Although we cannot produce the evangelistic fruits, we can participate in the evangelistic process. God saves, but He saves the lost through our involvement in evangelism. We are praying and working for His harvest. Realizing who produces the harvest reduces the pressure to win converts. We are successful when we tell someone about Jesus, regardless of the results. The Christian witness is accountable for participation, not for production.

What functions does prayer have in the life of a witness?

_____

_____

_____

Pray that God will give you His vision of the harvest as you train to be His witness.

Prepare Your Testimony
A basic tool for any Christian witness is an individual's story of what Jesus did for him or her. That story is called a per-

sonal testimony. Some people think that a testimony is effective only when it is dramatic or unusual. Fortunately, that is not the case. God is able to use any testimony as an evangelistic tool. To understand why, we will consider what makes a testimony effective.

A testimony is effective because it is a personal story. Unlike something heard or read, the personal testimony has been experienced. Since it is firsthand information, a testimony has unique authority. Lost people may not accept the authority of the Bible, but most will not deny the reality of a personal experience. Every testimony carries with it the authority of experience.

A personal testimony also arouses interest by allowing you to present the gospel in terms of what God did in your life. When you express the story of what Jesus did for you in a brief and interesting way, people will usually listen to the gospel.

You may choose from two types of personal testimonies:

1. A *salvation testimony* is the story of how you became a Christian.
2. A *recovery testimony* is the story of how Jesus helped you with a problem or a need in your life.

The principles involved in preparing your testimony for witnessing are simple:

Follow an outline. Using an outline keeps you on course in telling your story. Many people find that it also makes their testimonies easier to remember. Your experience can be outlined in many ways. One I have found helpful is:

• My life before Christ
• How I realized my need for Christ
• How I received Christ
• My life after receiving Christ

Write it out. Putting your testimony in written form will help you clarify what you want to say. It will also enable you to control the length of time you take to tell your story.

Use two specific statements to open and close your testimony. Begin by saying, "I have not always been a Christian." This gives you a common bond with each lost person you encounter. Your background and life-style may be different, but that statement means that you have shared the experience of being an unbeliever.

Close your testimony by asking, "Has anything like this ever happened to you?" If the person says no, ask permission to share the Roman Road to new life in Jesus. If the person says yes, ask him or her to share a testimony. If the testimony sounds unclear, you may still be able to share the gospel.

Keep it short. It is best to hold your testimony to two minutes or less.

Emphasize Jesus more than yourself. When you are writing your testimony, keep your focus clear. Sharing your testimony is not sharing your life story. It is telling the story of what Jesus did for you. Your purposes are to introduce Jesus and to explain briefly what He has done in your life.

Avoid Christianese. The most common problem of believers who use their testimonies to witness is Christianese. *Christianese* is a word coined to describe the language we use in church. Terms like *coming down the aisle* or *getting saved* have little meaning to persons who do not go to church. As you write your testimony, avoid using words and phrases unbelievers might not understand. When you use religious expressions, clarify them.

Using the suggested outline, write your testimony on another sheet of paper.

Find a Partner

When Jesus sent the disciples to minister, He sent them in pairs (see Luke 10:1). His model is still effective today. Witnessing with a partner has several benefits. One of the most important is an increased level of confidence. The presence of a partner means that you will have support when you witness. If you have a sense of inadequacy about witnessing, a partner makes it easier to have courage.

A partner can also strengthen your commitment to pray about personal evangelism. Persons who witness together pray together. As you share your needs with each other, you will find it natural to pray together. The witnessing partner will become a prayer partner.

Accountability and responsibility are further benefits of witnessing with another person. If a friend and I agree to witness together, I know I will follow through. Someone will be asking me to make evangelistic visits. Accountability usually results in productivity.

Look for a partner who is a member of your church. Prospects are easier to visit when both members of the witnessing team are from the same church. Your partner needs to be dependable. You will count on his or her faithfulness to encourage yours. Finally, the ideal partner is fully committed to the Lord and maintains a close walk with Him.

Seek the Spirit

The last aspect of preparation is the most important. To be ready to share your faith, seek the filling of the Holy Spirit. In Acts 1:8 Jesus told His disciples to be witnesses after the Holy Spirit came upon them. In Acts 4:18-21 the followers of Jesus were told that persecution would follow if they continued speaking about Jesus. After being filled with the Holy Spirit, however, they began to witness boldly in spite of the threats (see Acts 4:31). The Holy Spirit will help us overcome our fears and find a way to share the gospel.

A common misunderstanding about the filling of the Holy Spirit is that it refers to the coming of the Holy Spirit into our lives. In John 7:38-39 Jesus said that the Holy Spirit would be sent to those who believe in Him. The Holy Spirit comes into your life when you become a Christian. As you place your faith in Jesus, the Holy Spirit comes to dwell in you. According to Jesus, the indwelling is permanent (see John 14:16).

The filling of the Holy Spirit refers not to the Spirit's coming into our lives but to the Spirit's empowering us for witness and ministry. As we are filled with the Holy Spirit, we receive the courage and strength necessary to tell others about Jesus. Our lives and our lips become channels for the Spirit to use in spreading the gospel.

In Ephesians 5:18 Christians are commanded to "be filled with the Spirit." The Greek language reveals some important truths about this commandment. The verb is plural in form, indicating that the commandment is for all Christians. It is also an imperative verb, meaning that the action is required. Because it is a passive verb, the filling of the Spirit must be something God does for us. We cannot fill ourselves.

The command is also in the present tense. In the Greek language this indicates continuous action: "keep on being filled." Unlike salvation, the filling of the Spirit is not a one-time experience. Each time we go out to witness, we should seek to be filled with the Holy Spirit.

How can you be filled with the Spirit? Filling begins with *seeking*. In Matthew 7:7 Jesus said, " 'Ask and it will be given to you; seek and you will find; knock and the door will be opened to you.' " The Lord delights in giving to those who want to receive.

The next step is *cleansing* our hearts of all known sin. The Holy Spirit will not honor or bless a sinful life. The Bible tells us what to do about sin in 1 John 1:9: "If we confess our sins, he is faithful and just and will forgive us our sins and purify us from all unrighteousness." When our sin is forgiven and cleansed, we are ready to be filled.

The final step is *yielding* control of our lives to the Holy Spirit. When we accept His control, we will do His work. That work is to bear witness to Jesus (see John 15:26-27).

As we tell others about Jesus, we will experience the power and help of the Holy Spirit in three ways:

1. The Holy Spirit goes ahead of us to prepare the lost person to receive our witness (see John 16:8).
2. The Holy Spirit guides us in what to say and do as we witness (see Acts 1:8).
3. The Holy Spirit keeps our witness alive in the minds and souls of those who heard it (see John 15:26).

Follow the process of seeking, cleansing, and yielding as you prepare to witness. Describe how each step helps you experience the filling of the Holy Spirit.

Seeking:

_____
_____
_____
_____

Cleansing:

_____
_____
_____
_____

Yielding:

_____
_____
_____
_____

SHARE THE GOOD NEWS

Begin identifying and praying for lost persons you know.

Now that you have written your personal testimony (see p. 12), practice presenting it to a family member or your witnessing partner. Ask for suggestions for improving your presentation.

2 The Roman Road Witnessing Plan

Through the years, using a Bible or a New Testament to explain the plan of salvation has been one of the most popular and effective methods of witnessing. This approach is the one we will learn. The Roman Road will form the outline we will use to explain the gospel.

Selecting a New Testament

Begin by selecting a New Testament to use for personal evangelism. You will mark it by writing brief notes in the margins and by underlining key verses presenting the plan of salvation. Some people hesitate to mark in their Bibles from a fear that they are indicating disrespect for the Word of God. On the contrary, identifying a plan of salvation in the Bible offers it to the Holy Spirit for use in bringing the lost to salvation.

Marking the Roman Road in your Bible can help you lead persons to Christ in two ways. First, noting a plan of salvation on the pages of the Bible makes it easier for you to witness. When you underline the key verses and write brief notes in the margins, you do not have to remember as much. Your Bible or New Testament clearly identifies all the references you need to lead someone to Christ.

Second, marking your Bible makes it easier for a lost person to follow and understand your presentation of the gospel. The markings focus the attention of the unbeliever on the relevant truths about salvation. When someone is presented with a page of information, the natural tendency is to read the whole page. When one verse on that page is highlighted, however, he will look at the verse that stands out. This makes it easier to keep the conversation focused on what the Bible says about salvation.

You have three basic options in selecting a New Testament. Most Christians have one Bible they like to use regularly. You may choose to mark the New Testament in the Bible you use regularly. Since you use this Bible most of the time, you are likely to have it when you go to witness. Since you are more familiar with it, you may feel more comfortable in using it to tell persons how to be saved.

The use of a New Testament only is also a possibility. Its smaller size makes a New Testament easier to carry with you. You will tend to witness more often if your witnessing tool is available. The frequency factor is an important consideration. The more you witness, the more comfortable you will become in telling others about Jesus.

The third option is to mark an inexpensive New Testament that you plan to give away. Many persons do not have Bibles. When you share the gospel with someone who does not have a copy of the Scriptures, you may want to give the person a testament with an explanation of salvation already marked. If the individual does not accept Christ when you share with her, she may do so later as she studies the marked New Testament on her own. Your church may have some copies of the New Testament available for distribution to persons who need Bibles. If so, perhaps you could mark one or more of them with the Roman Road. An ideal New Testament for this purpose is *Here's Hope New Testament, Roman Road Edition.* This inexpensive edition, containing an easy-to-understand explanation of the plan of salvation, is available from LifeWay Church Resources Customer Service.[1]

You may consider marking all three types of Bibles. By marking the Bible you use most often, you will be exposed to the Roman Road repeatedly as you study your Bible for other purposes. This repetition makes it easier for you to learn. If you mark a small New Testament and carry it with you, you will tend to witness more often. Regular witnessing is the best way to develop confidence in your ability to explain the gospel to unbelievers. By marking inexpensive copies of the New Testament and giving them away, you can witness even when you are not present with the lost persons. The Holy Spirit can use the Roman Road when a person studies the plan of salvation on his own.

Which translation of the New Testament should you use? If you are using your Bible, the translation that is most meaningful to you will be acceptable. If you buy a New Testament for the specific purpose of witnessing, consider purchasing a contemporary translation, since it can be more easily understood by lost persons who lack Bible knowledge.

How many different Bibles and New Testaments do you have? _____

Indicate which one you want to mark with a plan of salvation and why you chose that version.

_____

_____

_____

_____

_____

_____

The Roman Road

When the Holy Spirit led Paul the apostle to write the letter we call Romans, one of His purposes seems to have been to provide a thorough discussion of salvation. Perhaps more than any other book of the Bible, Romans seeks to explain what salvation is, why salvation is necessary, and how salvation happens. This concern with salvation has made Romans a popular book to use in telling others about Jesus.

Over the years Christians involved in witnessing have found several verses in Romans to be a simple summary of the plan of salvation. The use of these verses was so effective and popular that they came to be called the Roman Road to salvation. Various versions of the Roman Road use different verses, but all of them use verses found in the Book of Romans. In learning the Roman Road, we will use eight passages from the Book of Romans. The following verses are from the *New International Version*, although any translation may be used effectively.

1. Romans 1:16: "I am not ashamed of the gospel, because it

is the power of God for the salvation of everyone who believes: first for the Jew, then for the Gentile."

2. Romans 2:4: "God's kindness leads you toward repentance."

3. Romans 3:23: "All have sinned and fall short of the glory of God."

4. Romans 5:8: "God demonstrates his own love for us in this: While we were still sinners, Christ died for us."

5. Romans 6:23: "The wages of sin is death, but the gift of God is eternal life in Christ Jesus our Lord."

6. Romans 10:9-10,13: "If you confess with your mouth, 'Jesus is Lord,' and believe in your heart that God raised him from the dead, you will be saved. For it is with your heart that you believe and are justified, and it is with your mouth that you confess and are saved. For, 'Everyone who calls on the name of the Lord will be saved.' "

7. Romans 8:16-17,38-39: "The Spirit himself testifies with our spirit that we are God's children. Now if we are children, then we are heirs—heirs of God and co-heirs with Christ, if indeed we share in his sufferings in order that we may also share in his glory. For I am convinced that neither death nor life, neither angels nor demons, neither the present nor the future, nor any powers, neither height nor depth, nor anything else in all creation, will be able to separate us from the love of God that is in Christ Jesus our Lord."

8. Romans 12:1-2: "I urge you, brothers, in view of God's mercy, to offer your bodies as living sacrifices, holy and pleasing to God—this is your spiritual act of worship. Do not conform any longer to the pattern of this world, but be transformed by the renewing of your mind. Then you will be able to test and approve what God's will is—his

good, pleasing and perfect will."

In this chapter you will mark your Bible for use in a witnessing encounter. The next chapter will explain the meaning of each passage in the Roman Road.

Marking Your Bible

To make it easier to share the Roman Road with someone, we will mark it in the Bible or the New Testament you have selected. If the one you plan to use does not have a margin wide enough for notes, write the entire outline inside the cover or on the front page.

1. Begin with the title page of your Bible or New Testament. Write the question *Can people in today's world have hope?* Under the question write the following cue phrase: *See Romans 1:16, page ___.* Fill in the blank page number with the page number of Romans 1:16 in your New Testament. For each point of the outline you will write both the reference and the page number in the New Testament to make the Scripture easy to find. This is how it should look:

Can people in today's world have hope?
See Romans 1:16, page 233

2. Find Romans 1:16 in your Bible and underline the verse. In the top margin of the page write: *God's power can make us secure.* In the bottom margin of the page write: *See Romans 2:4, page ___.*
3. Find Romans 2:4 in your Bible and underline the verse. In the top margin write: *God's power results in change.* In the bottom margin write: *See Romans 3:23, page ___.*
4. Find Romans 3:23 in your Bible and underline the verse.

In the top margin write: *Sin makes change necessary.* In the bottom margin write: *See Romans 5:8, page ___.*

5. Find Romans 5:8 in your Bible and underline the verse. In the top margin write: *God still loves us.* In the bottom margin write: *See Romans 6:23, page ___.*

6. Find Romans 6:23 in your Bible and underline the verse. In the top margin write: *Sin earns death, but God gives life.* In the bottom margin write: *See Romans 10:9-10,13, page ___.*

7. Find Romans 10:9-10,13 in your Bible and underline these verses. At the top of the page write: *Confess, repent, believe, call.* At the bottom of the page write: *Turn to back page.*

8. Turn to the back page or the inside cover of your Bible. At the top of the page write: *A Prayer for Salvation.* Then copy this prayer:

> Dear God, I know that Jesus is Your Son and that He died and was raised from the dead. Because I have sinned and need forgiveness, I ask Jesus to save me. I am willing to change the direction of my life by acknowledging Jesus as my Savior and Lord and by turning away from my sins. Thank You for giving me forgiveness, eternal life, and hope. In Jesus' name. Amen.

At the bottom of the page write: *See Romans 8:16-17,38-39, page ___.*

9. Find Romans 8:16-17,38-39 in your Bible and underline these verses. In the top margin write: *We now have hope.* In the bottom margin write: *See Romans 12:1-2, page ___.*

10. Find Romans 12:1-2 in your Bible and underline these verses. In the top margin write: *Faith = life for God.* In the bottom margin write: *Publicly profess your faith and be baptized. Read the Bible and pray daily. Tell others what God has done for you.*

Now you should have the outline of the Roman Road to salvation in your Bible or New Testament. Look back over it to be sure that you have a Scripture reference and a page number for each point. Often, you can lead someone to Christ by showing him the Roman Road.

Read each Scripture in your Bible and match it with the correct cue phrase.

___ 1. **Romans 10:9-10,13**	a.	**God's power can make us secure.**
___ 2. **Romans 3:23**		
___ 3. **Romans 8:16-17,38-39**	b.	**God's power results in change.**
___ 4. **Romans 6:23**		
___ 5. **Romans 1:16**	c.	**Sin makes change necessary.**
___ 6. **Romans 2:4**		
___ 7. **Romans 12:1-2**	d.	**God still loves us.**
___ 8. **Romans 5:8**	e.	**Sin earns death, but God gives life.**
	f.	**Confess, repent, believe, call.**
	g.	**We now have hope.**
	h.	**Faith = life for God.**

Check your answers by reviewing the material in this chapter.

A Prayer for Salvation

Many times persons who are lost and want to be saved do not know how to pray for salvation. The language used in prayer is not nearly as important as the attitude of the person praying. For many lost persons, however, even a simple and basic prayer is difficult to express.

If the lost person needs help praying, lead her through the prayer you recorded at the back of your Bible. Always clarify your role. Be sure that she understands that your words are not more holy or effective than hers. You are only helping her express what she wants Jesus to do in her life.

Every Christian should know how to lead someone in a prayer for salvation. Write one in your words.

_____

_____

_____

_____

Compare your prayer to the one you wrote at the back of your Bible as part of the Roman Road presentation. Remember that the language used is not the primary issue. The action of genuinely committing one's life to Christ matters most.

Using a Witnessing Booklet

Some witnesses prefer to use a gospel tract or a witnessing booklet to share the good news. This approach offers several advantages:
* You can read the explanation of the gospel.
* The outline will keep your conversation focused on salvation.

- You can leave the booklet with the person for review later or to share with others.

  If you use a witnessing booklet, follow these instructions:
- Use one copy so that you and the prospect can share and read together.
- Use your finger or a pen or a pencil to point out major truths.
- As you read the booklet, keep it folded so that you focus on one page at a time.

  How to Have a Full and Meaningful Life and *Here's Hope* are recommended tracts.[2]

Your New Testament is now ready to be used as a witnessing tool. The Roman Road to salvation is marked. A model prayer for salvation is recorded at the back.

SHARE THE GOOD NEWS

This week review the Roman Road process as you have recorded it in your Bible. Mentally practice following the outline with a lost person.

Continue to practice and improve your personal testimony with a family member or your witnessing partner.

Continue praying for lost persons you know.

---

[1]WRITE LifeWay Church Resources Customer Service; One LifeWay Plaza; Nashville, TN 37234-0113; FAX order to (615) 251-5933; PHONE (800) 458-2772; EMAIL to *customerservice@lifeway.com;* ORDER ONLINE at *www.lifeway.com;* or VISIT the LifeWay Christian Store serving you.
[2]Both tracts are available from LifeWay Church Resources Customer Service.

3 Understanding the Roman Road

Now that you have marked the Roman Road to salvation in your New Testament, you will want to learn how to use it effectively. To master the use of the Roman Road, you need to understand what each point means and to practice presenting it to others. We will begin with an explanation of what each verse means.

The Meaning of the Roman Road
Romans 1:16: God's power can make us secure. Many people today live without hope. They have no resources to strengthen them and guide them through their struggles in life. According to Romans 1:16, the focus of the Christian faith is God's power to help us in whatever problems we face. Through Jesus Christ a power great enough to bring salvation and deliverance is available. This power is not

just for people of a particular race or background. It is available to any person who believes.

> **Complete the statement: God's _____ can make us secure.**

Romans 2:4: God's power results in change. Through God's power, people can change. The biblical word for *change* is *repentance*. This means allowing God to change the direction of our lives.

> **Complete the statement: God's power results in _____.**

Romans 3:23: Sin makes change necessary. Why do people need to change? From what does Jesus offer deliverance? According to the Bible, every man and woman has a problem. The problem can be described in many ways, but the most common biblical word is *sin*. One meaning of *sin* is *to fall short of the mark God has set*. To understand what sin is, imagine an archer who aims his arrow at a target but misses. He may not have wanted to miss. He may have done his best to hit the target. In spite of his efforts, however, he missed the target.

The Bible teaches that God has a standard for us. That standard is perfection (see Matt. 5:48). The Lord expects each person to live a life of perfect obedience to Him. The failure to meet that standard is sin, which means that all people have a sin problem. We may do much that is good, and we may not want to do anything bad, but none of us can measure up to God's standard of always doing right.

Complete the statement: _____ makes change necessary.

How would you respond to someone who claims that he has done nothing wrong?

_____

_____

_____

_____

_____

_____

_____

_____

Romans 5:8: God still loves us. Some people think that our failure to meet God's standard or to hit God's mark means that God is our enemy. Because we do not live up to His expectations, God must be against us. But the message of Jesus is that in spite of our sin, God still loves us. That's good news!

God's love for us is not based on ignorance and on an unawareness of sin. Nor is His love based on a toleration that overlooks our sin. Knowing our sin, the Lord chose to love us, even though it meant the death of His Son for us. In doing what was necessary to overcome our problem with sin, God demonstrated the depth and reality of His love for us (also see John 3:16).

Complete the statement: God still _____ us.

Describe how you feel when you read this statement: Knowing our sin, the Lord chose to love us, even though

it meant the death of His Son for us.

_____

_____

_____

_____

_____

What effect will this truth have on your witnessing?

_____

_____

_____

_____

_____

Romans 6:23: Sin earns death, but God gives life. Sin would not be a problem if it did not have serious consequences. According to the Bible, the consequences of sin are too serious to overlook. Although God is not our enemy, He is our judge. As judge He cannot ignore our failure to "hit the target" with our lives. In Romans 6:23 we learn that "the wages of sin is death." Whenever we sin, we earn the wages of death. If every person is guilty of sin, then every person is subject to the consequences of eternal death and separation from God (see John 3:36; Rev. 20:11-15).

However, an alternative exists. Through our works we earn death, but "the gift of God is eternal life in Christ Jesus our Lord" (Rom. 6:23). Jesus died on the cross in our place (see 1 Pet. 3:18). He took our guilt for sin upon Himself so that His death would fulfill the judgment of God against our sin (see 2 Cor. 5:21; Col. 2:13-14). Our sin is judged in the death of Jesus on the cross as our substitute. By our works we earn death, but by His grace we can receive eternal life.

God offers eternal life and the forgiveness of sin through Jesus Christ as a gift.

> **Complete the statement: Sin earns _____, but God gives _____.**

The Call to Salvation

Romans 10:9-10,13: Confess, repent, believe, call. These four words summarize what someone must do to receive God's free gift and be saved.

The biblical word translated *confess* means *to say the same thing. Lord* may be translated *ruler, boss,* or *sovereign authority.* When we confess Jesus as Lord, we are saying the same thing about God that He says about Himself (see Isa. 45:5-7,22-24; Phil. 2:10-11). We recognize His rightful authority over us. In acknowledging Jesus as Lord, we admit our sin in failing to "hit the mark" of perfect obedience and righteousness.

> **Confessing Jesus as Lord means that we recognize His rightful _____ over us.**

To confess Jesus as Lord also means to *repent* of our sins. In accepting His authority over us, we turn away from life on our terms in order to obey and serve Him. This turning away from sin in order to follow Jesus is called repentance. More than feeling sorry, it is changing the direction of our lives and living a God-oriented rather than a self-oriented life (see Luke 3:7-14).

> **Repentance means changing the _____ of our lives and living a _____ life.**

Believe means *to trust*. When you "believe in your heart
that God raised him from the dead" (Rom. 10:9), you have
confidence that the death and resurrection of Jesus are
enough to secure your salvation. You trust in the work of
Christ rather than in the work of your life for your salvation.
When you look at a bridge, you might know that it would
hold you up if you crossed it. The bridge never actually
holds you up, however, until you get on it and cross.
Similarly, you may know a lot about Jesus, but until you
trust Him with your life, putting your life into His hands, you
are not believing in Him. To believe in Jesus is to put your
life, both physically and spiritually, into His hands.

**Believing means _____ Jesus with
your life.**

When we acknowledge that Jesus is the rightful Lord or
boss of our lives and when we are willing to believe in Him,
trusting in His work alone for our salvation, we need only
call on Him to be saved. In Romans 10:13 Paul wrote,
" 'Everyone who calls on the name of the Lord will be
saved.' " Note how broad the invitation is. *Anyone* who is
willing to call on the name of the Lord will be saved. No
other qualifications are needed. If you are willing to call on
Him, you can be saved.

To call on the name of the Lord is to ask Him for
forgiveness of sin and for salvation. When you ask Him for
salvation, you are acknowledging Him as your Lord and
expressing your intention to live a life of obedience and
service. Persons who call on Him will be saved. The sinner's
prayer that you recorded at the back of your New Testament
is an example of a prayer for salvation that you can use.

Calling on the name of the Lord means asking **Him** for _____ of sin and for

_____.

At this point you will want to ask the person hearing the gospel if he wants to call on the Lord and be saved. If he says yes, tell him how to pray for salvation. Use the prayer you recorded at the back of your Bible if you wish. After the person prays to receive Christ, lead him in a prayer to thank God for what He has done for him.

The four words that summarize what someone must do to be saved are: _____, _____,

_____, _____.

Romans 8:16-17,38-39: We now have hope. When we are saved, God adopts us as His children, and His Holy Spirit assures us that we are part of His family. According to Roman law at the time of Paul's writing, someone's adopted son also became his heir. While Christ is God's heir by nature, Christians have become God's heirs by adoption. Therefore, we are joint-heirs with Christ.

Verses 38-39 tell us that we are eternally secure in God. Because Christ has defeated the principalities and powers of this earth, we need not fear human and superhuman enemies. Nothing can separate us from God's love in Christ Jesus.

Believers can live with hope because they are children of God and are secure in His love.

Complete the statement: We now have _____.

Romans 12:1-2: Faith = life for God. When you become a Christian, you begin to live your life for God. When you lead persons to Christ, use these verses to indicate some ways their lives will change.

A new Christian can expect her life to be different. God wants a person's life to change as she follows Jesus, even if it means sacrifice. The goal for believers is to look and live less like the unsaved people of the world and more like Jesus. That kind of change happens because God brings it about. He will transform the new Christian's life, making it more like the life of Jesus (see Phil. 1:6; 2:13). You don't have to be religiously inclined to become a faithful Christian. Jesus will make you look and live like one of His children.

Complete the statement: Faith = life for _____.

List ways a Christian's life is different from an unsaved person's life.

_____

_____

_____

_____

_____

_____

_____

_____

Take action. A new Christian needs to follow up his decision by taking several steps. Encourage him to profess his faith publicly in a church, then to be baptized. Tell him to share with others what Christ has done for him. Finally, help him become involved in a fellowship of growing Christians and to learn more about his relationship with God through daily prayer, Bible study, and discipleship.

Practicing the Roman Road

By now you should understand the verses used in the Roman Road. To deepen your understanding and to learn the Road better, you need to practice explaining the Roman Road to someone else.

It is best to practice with another Christian who is interested in witnessing. You don't have to worry about your performance, because that person is also trying to learn. Find a partner. Using your marked New Testament, go through the Roman Road and explain it as you would to a lost person. Be sure to include leading the sinner's prayer as a part of your practice. When you have gone through all of the Roman Road, ask your partner for comments or suggestions about improving your presentation. Change roles and let your partner practice sharing the Roman Road with you.

Also practice sharing the Roman Road outside the study. If possible, practice at least once with a member of your family. Ask your family member to help you with a study assignment. Tell him to listen as if he were an unbeliever and to ask questions if something is not clear. When you complete your explanation of the Roman Road, ask for questions or comments about the presentation.

Preparing flash cards is another way to learn the Roman Road. Get eight index cards of any size. Using a card for each reference, on one side write the Scripture reference and on the other write the key word or phrase from the margin of your New Testament. The card for the first stop on the Roman Road would have *Romans 1:16* on one side and *God's power can make us secure* on the other side.

Read through the index cards as often as you can. Ask Christian friends or family members to help you review by asking you questions about the cards. If you will write the full verse under the reference and review it often, you will be surprised by how easily you are able to memorize the Roman Road.

By now you should be familiar with the Roman Road. The more you share it with others, the more comfortable you will become with witnessing.

After practicing the Roman Road, try matching the Scripture references and the cue phrases without finding the verses in your Bible.

___ 1. **Romans 10:9-10,13**
___ 2. **Romans 3:23**
___ 3. **Romans 8:16-17,38-39**
___ 4. **Romans 6:23**
___ 5. **Romans 1:16**
___ 6. **Romans 2:4**
___ 7. **Romans 12:1-2**
___ 8. **Romans 5:8**

a. **God's power can make us secure.**
b. **God's power results in change.**
c. **Sin makes change necessary.**
d. **God still loves us.**
e. **Sin earns death, but God gives life.**
f. **Confess, repent, believe, call.**
g. **We now have hope.**
h. **Faith = life for God.**

Check your answers by reviewing the material in this chapter.

SHARE THE GOOD NEWS

The goal of practice is to prepare you for an actual experience. To learn the Roman Road adequately, you need to share it with someone who is not a Christian. Think of a friend, an acquaintance, or a relative who is an unbeliever. As soon as possible, ask the person to help you with a study assignment. Tell her that you are studying to learn how to explain the Christian faith in a brief, simple, and clear manner. Ask the person to allow you a few moments to present what you have learned and to answer questions.

After you explain Romans 10:9-10,13, ask your friend if what you have shared makes sense to her. If you get a positive response, ask the person if she wants to become a Christian. If the answer is yes, show her how to receive God's gift of salvation. If the answer is no, thank her for allowing you to share. Be sure to find out if she has any comments or questions about your presentation.

4 Visiting and Cultivating a Prospect

Three ingredients are necessary for developing confidence in witnessing: training, practice, and experience. You have had training and practice. To get the experience that makes the training and practice useful, you must go and tell others about Jesus.

Identifying Evangelistic Prospects

Generally, we can identify three types of prospects for your church. *Church-member prospects* are Christians but are not presently involved in a church. Your church will want to reach and involve these persons. *Ministry prospects* are persons who need some type of ministry. Although they are Christians and may be church members, they are inactive. They may have spiritual, emotional, or family problems that prevent their involvement in church and their growth in the

Christian life. Your church can find ways to minister to and encourage these persons.

The prospects whose needs you are training to meet are known as *evangelistic prospects*. Although they may have other problems and needs, their primary need is salvation. Through a relationship with Jesus, you can help these persons find hope, forgiveness, and eternal life.

The challenge facing the Christian witness and the church is to find evangelistic prospects. In Mark 4:1-20 Jesus used a parable to show that the work of the Christian witness is like farming. The Christian who witnesses is like a farmer who plants seed. All of the seeds that are planted may not produce fruit, but some of the seeds planted will always produce fruit. The keys to producing fruit are to keep planting seeds and to plant them in the best possible soil.

Discovering evangelistic prospects is a twofold task. We must find the prospects and then determine whether those prospects are ready for the gospel. We want to witness to all evangelistic prospects in ways that are appropriate to their interest in the gospel.

The SEED Approach

One way to find and analyze unsaved prospects is called the SEED approach. *SEED* stands for the four steps involved in finding and analyzing prospects: search, encounter, evaluate, and decide.

Search. To find prospects, you must look for them. Start by developing a list of the evangelistic prospects you know personally.

List the names of lost persons you know in the following categories.

- **Immediate family:** _____

  _____

- **Other relatives:** _____

  _____

- **Friends:** _____

  _____

- **Work colleagues:** _____

  _____

- **Neighbors:** _____

  _____

- **Acquaintances:** _____

  _____

Now add contact information such as telephone numbers or addresses under the names.

Also examine church records for unsaved prospects:
- Unsaved Sunday School members
- Unsaved family members and relatives of church members
- Unsaved parents of children and youth
- Worship-service visitors

Encounter. The next step is to verify the information you have and to determine the evangelistic need and potential of each prospect. Use the telephone to make encounter contacts, since you can make several calls in a short period of time.

When you call, ask to speak to the prospect. Introduce yourself by giving your name and your church's name. State that you are conducting a brief survey of some persons in the community. If you are given permission, verify the address you have and ask the following questions:

1. "What family members live with you?"
2. "What are your interests and hobbies?"
3. "Do you know anyone who is a member of our church? Whom?"

At this point tell the person that you have only two more questions.

4. "Do you know for certain that you have eternal life and will go to heaven when you die?"
5. "If God asked you, 'Why should I let you into heaven?' what would you say?"

When you have finished, thank the person for answering the questions.

Evaluate. The next step in the process is to evaluate the evangelistic potential of the prospects you encountered. Answer the following questions for each prospect.

What is the prospect's connection with the church? If the connection with the church is a personal relationship, the prospect may be more open to hearing the gospel and to becoming a Christian and a church member. If the connection is attendance at a worship service or another church event, the prospect has indicated at least some degree of interest in spiritual matters. A prospect with a connection from a visit or a survey may need to be involved in various church activities to build relationships with Christians and to hear the gospel in different forms.

What is the prospect's spiritual condition? The encounter call may reveal that the person is a Christian who is out of fellowship with God or an unaffiliated Christian who needs a church home. If it is determined that some are not evangelistic prospects, add them to the file for church-member prospects or ministry prospects.

What is the person's spiritual interest? Does the prospect have some or no understanding of the gospel? If he is interested but not yet ready to make a commitment to Christ, his evangelistic potential may be high. If he is uninterested or does not allow you to share, his potential may be low now. In this case a patient process of cultivation is needed.

What interests or needs did you discover? How can you and your church help? The gospel needs to be shared and explained to all lost persons, but it also needs to be illustrated in the ways we meet specific needs.

In light of the information you have gathered, how would you rate the evangelistic potential of the prospect?

Evaluate the evangelistic potential of the following prospects by labeling them good, fair, or long-range.

1. **A single adult who attends regularly and has friends in the church: _____**
2. **An adult found through a survey with no previous connection with the church: _____**
3. **A teenager who attended a pizza party at church: _____**
4. **A young couple who, with their new baby, visited the church three times last month: _____**

Decide. The final step is to develop a witnessing strategy for each evangelistic prospect. Start with the prospects who have the highest evangelistic potential.

Use a prayer list. Make a list of persons you want to win to Christ and begin to pray for them each day. Pray that the Holy Spirit will open their minds and hearts to the gospel. Pray that they will recognize their need for salvation. Pray that they will hear something about Jesus from every Christian who knows them. Also pray for God's wisdom and direction as you seek to share the gospel with them.

Make a visit. Set a time to go and witness to them. Remember to go with a witnessing partner. In the next section we will discuss making an evangelistic visit in someone's home. When you go, be prepared to share your testimony and the Roman Road.

Find a need and begin to meet it. If you share an interest with the prospect, use it to build a relationship.

Introduce the prospect to other Christians. Look for ways to minister to her and to illustrate the love of Christ for her.

Set a Time

The best way to get witnessing experience is to set a time each week for evangelistic visitation. When you have a definite time to witness, you know you will witness at least once each week. Honor your scheduled time like a doctor's appointment or a business meeting. Don't let other demands crowd out a time to share Christ with persons who are lost.

When you and your partner set a time to go together, you will visit regularly with someone else who thinks that sharing Christ is important. This will strengthen your commitment to tell others about Jesus. If your church has a weekly visitation program, go at that time. You will be encouraged by meeting with others who want to make witnessing a priority.

Complete the following sentences.

The best time for me to visit evangelistically is
_____.

The person I would most like to be my witnessing partner is _____.
I can start regular evangelistic visitation on
_____.

With experience you will find it more and more natural to share your faith in Christ. When you share the gospel on a regular basis, personal witnessing becomes a habit.

State Your Purpose
The guidelines for going to someone's home to witness are more common sense than sophisticated technique. If possible, call the person to set up an appointment. When you arrive, park your car legally. Do not park in the driveway unless it is the only place to park. Having to move your car to let someone in or out can cause an awkward interruption in your presentation. After you knock on the door or ring the doorbell, step back away from the door to appear as nonthreatening as possible.

When someone answers the door, introduce yourself and your partner. State the purpose of your visit and identify whom you came to see. Call the person by name without referring to a prospect card so that the person at the door does not wonder what else you have on the card and where you got your information.

If you were going to make a witnessing visit to John Smith, you might introduce yourself like this: "Hello. My name is Chuck Kelley, and this is Jack Hunter. We are from First

Baptist Church and came to visit with John Smith for a few minutes. If John is available, could we come in and chat with him?" In a few seconds you have introduced yourself, indicated the spiritual nature of your visit, identified whom you came to see, and asked permission to come in. You may use other ways to introduce yourself, but be sure to cover these matters at the door.

If you are invited in, you have permission to talk with John about spiritual matters. If the prospect is unavailable, ask for a suggestion of a good time to return.

Tell Your Story
When you go to visit an evangelistic prospect, keep two goals in mind. One is to share the gospel. The other is to make a friend. To make a friend, you need to get to know something about a person. That is the purpose of the first part of your conversation. Begin by complimenting some feature of the prospect's home or yard.

Friends always know about each other's family and background. You will want to ask about the person's family, occupation, and interests or hobbies. Some of this information may be on the prospect card, but let the one you are visiting tell you himself. When you notice similarities between the prospect and you, point them out. Remember that you are building a relationship.

Your testimony is the bridge between the relational phase and the witnessing phase of the conversation. Telling the story of what Jesus did for you can open the door for you to present the Roman Road. To make the transition, tell the prospect that you would like to share briefly the most important thing that ever happened to you. Then tell your story.

Here is one example of how to make that transition in a conversation: "John, I came here tonight with two goals in mind. One was to get to know you, and I have enjoyed finding out a little bit about you. The other goal was to tell you about the greatest thing that ever happened to me. I haven't always been a Christian." At that point you begin telling your story.

Share the Roman Road
Your personal testimony will lead naturally to an opportunity to share the Roman Road. Use the end of your testimony to seek permission to share the gospel. The last sentence of your testimony should be the question "Has anything like this ever happened to you?" If the answer is yes, ask the person to share his story with you. If the testimony is clear, you can talk about church membership. If it is unclear, you may still need to share the gospel.

An illustration of how to handle a response of yes, followed by an unclear testimony, is: "Thank you for sharing your story with us, John. May I get your reaction to something? Have you ever heard of the Roman Road? The Roman Road is a brief summary of how people can have hope in today's world. I marked it here in my New Testament. As you can see, it begins in Romans 1:16 with an explanation of God's intent to help us." At this point you are beginning the presentation.

If you ask, "Has anything like this ever happened to you?" and the person says no, ask him to allow you to present the Roman Road. Here is an example of what to say after a response of no: "John, if nothing like that ever happened to you, I really have some good news. Let me show you something called the Roman Road. The Roman Road is a brief explanation of how people can have hope in today's world. I marked it in my Bible so that you can read with me. As you can see, it begins by stating God's intent to help us." Then continue the presentation.

> Try role-playing a visit in someone's home. Let a partner play the unbeliever. Start from your knock on the door and go through the first point on the Roman Road.

When you are planning to witness by sharing the Roman Road, remember these simple guidelines.

- Build a relationship as you share the gospel. Your warmth and courtesy will strengthen your witness and will open the door for further contact.
- Use your testimony as the bridge to the presentation.
- Using your marked New Testament, point to the verses and phrases to help focus the prospect's attention.

Secure a Decision

The goal of every witnessing experience is the conversion of the prospect. For that to happen, you must bring the person to a point of decision. The person may say yes or no to Jesus, but a decision should be made.

You will give the prospect the opportunity to make a decision for Christ after you explain Romans 10:9-10,13. After you have explained this passage, ask the person, "Does what we have been talking about make sense to you?" If he says no, find out what he does not understand and clarify it. If he says yes, tell him that a choice must be made between the wage we earn, which is death, and the free gifts God offers, which are forgiveness and new life through Jesus. Ask which alternative he would like to choose.

If he wants to receive God's gift of eternal life in Jesus, review the Romans 10 passage and show him how to call on the Lord for salvation. After the prayer for salvation lead in a prayer of thanksgiving and show the new believer the rest of the Roman Road.

The Holy Spirit is the One who produces an awareness of sin and a hunger for salvation. When the prospect does not want to receive God's gift of forgiveness and eternal life, ask if he does not understand an issue. If so, discuss it as the situation allows. If the person is simply unwilling to make a commitment, it may mean that the Holy Spirit has not yet convicted him of his need for salvation or that he is fighting against the Holy Spirit. Remember that God may use a number of witnesses to bring this person to an eventual commitment. Each witness you have with the unbeliever is important, regardless of its immediate outcome. Begin cultivating the person for a future commitment to Christ.

Start Cultivation

When a prospect says no to Christ after a presentation of the gospel, follow these steps to cultivate the relationship.

Leave the door open for another conversation about the gospel. Thank the person for allowing you to share the Roman Road. If possible, leave a marked New Testament or a witnessing tract with the person and encourage her to read it carefully and to think further about her relationship with God. Ask permission to lead a prayer seeking God's guidance for her as she considers the message of Jesus. As you are leaving, tell the prospect that you will look forward to a later opportunity to talk about her relationship with God. Thank her again for giving you the opportunity to spend some time with her.

Make other contacts with the prospect. Begin by writing her a brief note to express how much you enjoyed the visit. Mention again that you are looking forward to another opportunity to talk. A handwritten note is best. If you know her birthday or anniversary, send a card on the appropriate date. From time to time make a telephone call to see how she and her family are doing.

Find ways to meet a need or to encourage an interest. If you learn of an illness, of the birth of a child, or of another family need, respond with a card, a visit, or another form of help and encouragement. Use the person's interests to strengthen your relationship. If John is a lost prospect, and you both have an interest in golf, invite him to play sometime. Suggest that each of you bring a friend. This will probably make him more comfortable, and it might give you a chance to meet another prospect.

Involve the prospect in activities that will expose him to the gospel and that will give him an opportunity to meet other Christians. Invite the person to special church activities that will appeal to his interests. As a person hears the gospel in different ways and spends more time around Christians, he will become more open to the Christian faith.

Throughout the process of cultivation talk about Jesus whenever you have an opportunity. Every conversation does not need to be a gospel presentation, but stay in touch with the person's thinking about God. Make occasional visits for the sole purpose of witnessing. Let your witnessing partner share his testimony. Use an evangelistic tract to present the gospel. Engage in dialogue about any religious questions the person might have. Remember the two purposes of cultivation. You want the prospect to know that you truly care about him, and you want him to know that you are always willing to talk with him about the Lord.

Be persistent. When a seed is planted and cultivated, it usually produces fruit. When you share the gospel and continue cultivating it, the harvest of conversion will come.

> **Write what you would include in a note to someone you visited who did not accept Christ.**

_____

_____

_____

_____

_____

_____

_____

_____

_____

_____

_____

_____

SHARE THE GOOD NEWS

Share as the Lord leads you with a lost person this week.

Make a list of several lost persons whom you want to cultivate. Beside their names write specific steps you will take to cultivate these relationships.

5 Overcoming Barriers to Witnessing

When I teach classes and lead seminars in evangelism, the topic that interests most people is how to handle objections and questions. The common desire is to learn answers to every question you will face as you talk to others about Christ. That is an unrealistic and unnecessary goal. As you share the gospel, you will often be asked questions that you have not encountered before.

The best way to overcome barriers in witnessing is to learn principles you can use to deal with any problem that arises. We will consider some basic approaches for dealing with the barriers you are likely to face as a witness for Christ.

The Personal Barrier

The most difficult barrier to overcome is formed by hindrances in our personal lives. Other barriers come as we are engaged in the task of telling others about Jesus, but this barrier keeps us from starting to share. Among the hindrances that form this barrier are fear, time, apathy, and a general sense of inadequacy.

Fear. Fear about witnessing takes many forms: the fear of rejection, the fear of what others will think, the fear of forcing your views on others, and so on. The key to overcoming the barrier of fear is faith. The psalmist wrote:

> The Lord is my light and my salvation—
> whom shall I fear?
> The Lord is the stronghold of my life—
> of whom shall I be afraid? (Ps. 27:1).

You can deal with fear by claiming a Bible promise about God's power to care for you as you witness. Other promises are Isaiah 41:10; Jeremiah 32:17; Acts 1:8; and 1 Peter 5:6-7.

Time. Time is a hindrance to witnessing, as well as to many other activities in our lives. As with money, we never seem to have enough. But if we wait until we have time to witness, that time will never come. The key to dealing with the hindrance of time is obedience. Jesus commanded His followers to be witnesses (see Matt. 28:18-20; John 20:21). If He is our Lord, we must obey. We are to make time for witnessing and build our schedule around it. The obedient Christian will do whatever it takes to make time to share the gospel.

Apathy. Apathy is a personal barrier for those who do not feel that they need to witness. Some feel that it is a job for others to do. Others believe that it is not an urgent task. Their attitude seems to be that it is nice when people come to Christ, but it is not the end of the world when they don't. The key to overcoming apathy is compassion. People without Christ will spend eternity in hell. People without Christ do not have God's help in the struggle of daily living. If we truly care about others, we will want them to hear about Jesus.

A sense of inadequacy. A personal hindrance felt to some degree by all is a sense of inadequacy about sharing the gospel. Some of us feel that we don't know enough. Others think that we might do more harm than good. The issue, however, is not what we are capable of doing but what God is capable of doing. Understanding our role is the key to dealing with a sense of inadequacy. We are to be witnesses, telling others what Christ has done for us and can do for them. God's roles are to convince the unsaved that what we say is true and to transform them into Christians. We may not be spiritual giants or brilliant theologians, but we can be witnesses about the work of Jesus in our lives.

Every Christian faces hindrances in his life and feelings that discourage him from witnessing. The best way to overcome any personal barrier is to get involved in telling others about Jesus. As you witness, you will find yourself becoming more confident and committed to sharing Christ.

What are the greatest personal barriers you face as you consider involvement in witnessing? As you list each, pray for God's direction in dealing with it.

_____

_____

_____

The Distraction Barrier

When you overcome the personal barrier that keeps you from witnessing, you may find that other barriers hinder you in sharing the gospel. One of these is distraction. What do you do when you are attempting to share the gospel and something happens to arrest the attention of the prospect? Interruptions can come in any number of ways: a child demanding attention, a dog barking, a television blaring, or persons entering the room while you are talking.

Expect distractions to happen. Do unexpected things happen in your home? Telephones ring, babies cry, and conversations are interrupted in most homes on most days. Most distractions are not unusual. They are probably bigger distractions for you than for the person with whom you are sharing. A significant distraction for you may be a daily routine in the home you are visiting.

Be patient in making your presentation. An interruption does not mean that the conversation is over. It may only mean waiting to get the person's attention again. When the situation is resolved, pick up the conversation with a brief reminder of what was said and then move on to your next point.

Involve your partner in dealing with the distraction. One of the important reasons for visiting with a partner is to have help when distractions occur. The one who is not witnessing should plan to do what is necessary to help. That may mean playing on the floor with a child or giving the pet some attention. In any case, the partner should look for opportunities to minimize distractions.

Ask the person for help. Never underestimate the routine nature of most distractions. The person with whom you are sharing may not notice that what is happening makes the conversation difficult. For example, if the television is on, you could say: "Would you mind if we turned down the television a bit? I am having a little trouble hearing you." On most occasions the person will then turn it off.

The principle to remember is this: Keep sharing unless circumstances develop that make it impossible or inappropriate to continue. In this event conclude the conversation with warmth and courtesy and express your interest in returning at a better time. You might say something like this: "I can see that this is not a very good time for us to visit, Mrs. Smith. Thank you for your time. We will come back at a more convenient time for you."

Classify the following distractions as normal (N) or unusual (U).

_____ 1. **A small child climbing in and out of a mother's lap**
_____ 2. **The arrival of guests from out of town**
_____ 3. **A telephone call**
_____ 4. **A loud television**

How would you handle these distractions if they happened while you were witnessing?

1. _____
2. _____
3. _____
4. _____

The Objection Barrier
The gospel is confrontational. In 1 Corinthians 1:23 Paul

described the response he encountered in sharing the gospel: "We preach Christ crucified: a stumbling block to Jews and foolishness to Gentiles." When people hear the gospel, they may raise questions or voice objections as they come to grips with its demands.

The Christian witness need not fear questions and objections for several reasons. You will have divine guidance. In Matthew 10:19-20 Jesus promised that persons faced with unexpected demands will be guided by the Holy Spirit. Even when you do not have an answer for a question, the Holy Spirit will help you know what to say or do next.

Also, people raise questions or voice objections only if they are interested and involved in the conversation. The person who asks you a question is listening to you. The apathetic person uninterested in what you are saying is harder to deal with than someone who is asking questions about God.

Questions carry a personal benefit, as well. As you witness, the questions you face will stimulate your spiritual growth. Any teacher knows that the task of explaining always makes matters clearer to the one who explains. A few guidelines will help you handle the questions you face.

Handle questions or objections as they arise. If a later part of the Roman Road will answer the question, explain that you will be dealing with that issue in a moment. Make sure the person knows that you hear him and are interested in his response. No one likes to be ignored.

Maintain the tone of a discussion and not of a debate. You have not come to win argument. You have come to share Christ. Although you should be prepared to give a reasonable explanation of what you believe, you do not have to be able to prove your point beyond any shadow of doubt.

The responsibility of the witness is expressed well in 1 Peter 3:15: "In your hearts set apart Christ as Lord. Always be prepared to give an answer to everyone who asks you to give the reason for the hope that you have. But do this with gentleness and respect."

Keep the conversation focused on the individual's relationship with God. When people get into a religious conversation, they sometimes want to use it as a format to discuss all types of religious questions. If someone asks you a question unrelated to salvation, acknowledge the question and ask if it is an issue affecting the person's relationship with God. If it is, discuss it. If not, suggest that you come back to it after you explain the Roman Road. You can avoid digressions by evaluating questions in light of the person's relationship with God.

Do not be afraid to say, "I have not thought about that" or "I don't know." If you don't present yourself as an expert in theology, people will not expect you to be one. Questions may arise for which you and your partner are unable to give satisfying answers. At that point acknowledge the validity of the question, ask for some time to consider it, and seek to move back to the Roman Road. Here is one way to handle such a situation: "John, that is an interesting question, and it deserves a better response than I can give off the top of my head. I would like to give it some thought and meet with you again to talk about it. Before I leave, however, could I show you the rest of the Roman Road?"

Most people will appreciate your honesty and your interest and will allow you to finish the Roman Road. This situation can be very helpful because it gives you a reason to make another visit. Always follow through when you promise to come back to talk about an issue.

The Hostility Barrier

Many Christians dread witnessing because they fear running into a person who will react in a harsh and hostile manner. My experience, from witnessing on streets and beaches to home visitation, indicates that a hostile reaction to a witness is very rare. What should you do if you have one of those rare experiences? Respond with courtesy and warmth. God's love, not a person's response, should determine how we react. Often we receive from others the attitude we give to them.

If your witnessing effort is met with hostility, apologize for any interruption or inconvenience caused by your visit. You may have come at a bad time and elicited a response that was out of character. As you leave, offer your services and those of your church if the person should ever have a need. After the visit write a note to the person. Apologize again for any inconvenience or misunderstanding caused by your visit and express your interest in the person's well-being.

To cultivate a person like this, look for ways to meet needs. Nothing changes hostility like love expressed in meeting needs. Do something for the person even if you cannot witness, and you might have an opportunity to witness later. People who begin with an open hostility to the gospel can become very responsive as time passes. Consistent love and concern, expressed over time in the face of open hostility and rejection, can become very powerful witnesses.

Christians who are obedient to the Lord's command to witness will experience various hindrances as they share Christ with others. The Lord is faithful, however, and He will supply whatever is necessary to enable you to share Christ. Through the power of the Holy Spirit you can overcome any barrier and can be an effective witness for Jesus: "You, dear children, are from God and have overcome them, because the one who is in you is greater than the one who is in the world" (1 John 4:4).

List three things you could do to build a relationship with someone who was hostile when you attempted to witness.

_____

_____

_____

_____

_____

_____

SHARE THE GOOD NEWS
Pray about any barriers you have encountered in witnessing. This week take specific steps to work on these hindrances and continue to witness as the Lord leads you.

6

Following Through with New Christians

The work of a Christian witness is not over once he has led someone to Christ. In many ways it is just beginning. The Bible describes the process of conversion as a new birth (see John 3:3). As a new child needs assistance to grow and develop, so a spiritual baby (a new Christian) needs help to grow and develop into a mature believer. We will learn what to do after you have led someone to Christ.

Finish the Roman Road

The last two stops on the Roman Road are to be shared with new Christians. You will use Romans 8:16-17,38-39 to assure them that they are children of God and are secure in His love, no matter what trials they face in life.

You will use Romans 12:1-2 to show new Christians how

Christ should affect their lives. Christians are to live in a way pleasing to God. The better one gets to know Jesus, the more like Jesus one should become. The source of our values, attitudes, and actions should be the Christ within us and not the world around us.

Important Tools
You will find several tools helpful in doing follow-up work. A few of them will be identified here. Get other suggestions from your pastor or from other church-staff members.

The Bible. The Bible is the first and the most essential tool. Since most believers have several copies of the Bible, we sometimes assume that everyone has a Bible. On the contrary, many people do not own copies of God's Word. Each time you lead someone to Christ, ask the person if she has the Bible in a translation she can understand. Some will need Bibles. Others may have Bibles but in translations that are difficult for them to follow.

If a Bible is needed, give one to the new believer. Giving it as a gift from the church is a good way to illustrate the love and concern of your congregation. If possible, churches should keep inexpensive copies of the Bible or of the New Testament available for distribution to persons who need them. As a general rule, contemporary translations are easier for new Christians to use.

Welcome to God's Family. A second tool for helping new Christians is titled *Welcome to God's Family,*[1] a tract for new Christians. In a brief and colorful format it presents the basic information new Christians need to know. Among the topics covered are the assurance of salvation, steps for spiritual growth, and some information about the importance of baptism and church membership.

Introduce the tract after you finish the Roman Road. You could say something like this: "John, we are happy and excited about your commitment tonight. Before we leave, we want to show you a special tract that was written for new Christians like you. It will be yours to keep." Go through it by reading each page with the person and by answering any questions. Put your name and telephone number and the name and number of the church on the back.

Survival Kit . A third tool for follow-up is *Survival Kit*.[2] This resource is a workbook that accompanies the new Christian's Bible study. Earlier we learned that the Bible can be an intimidating Book for new believers. *Survival Kit* teaches new Christians how to study the Bible and how to grow spiritually. The format is an interactive Bible study using learning activities and Scripture to make the sessions interesting and easy to follow. Topics include the church, the old nature-new nature conflict, salvation, authority, and witnessing. It is designed for a person to complete as an individual, daily study.

Mention *Survival Kit* at the end of your witnessing visit and bring it to the convert at another time. This gives you a reason for future contacts with the new Christian. As you leave, you can say: "We would like to come by next week and bring a free book from our church. It will help you learn how to study the Bible and will teach you more about the Christian faith." After you deliver *Survival Kit*, check on the person's progress from time to time to see if you can offer assistance. Strongly encourage all new Christians to complete the entire study individually or in a group. Editions of *Survival Kit* for adults (English, Spanish and Korean editions), youth, and children (English and Spanish editions) are available.

If you do not use *Welcome to God's Family* or *Survival Kit*, use your New Testament to deal with a very important issue. On the back page of your New Testament write: *Assurance of salvation: 1 John 5:13; John 10:28.* Turn to the verses and underline them.

God wants all Christians to know for certain that they have eternal life. Our certainty is not based on the greatness of our faith. Assurance of salvation comes from the authority of God's Word and the promise of Jesus. First John 5:13 confirms our salvation. If we have followed God's guidelines, we have God's salvation. John 10:28 reminds us that salvation is the result of what Jesus does for us. Because of what Jesus does for us, we can know that we have been and always will be saved.

Other Christians. Relationships are some of the most important follow-up tools for the new Christian. You will want to do all you can to help the new convert meet other Christians. Many new believers have few Christian friends. They will need support and encouragement as they learn to follow Jesus. When new Christians come to church, help them meet people and make friends. Include the convert in social gatherings and special events at the church. Developing Christian friendships will encourage a new believer to grow spiritually and to become active in church.

Christian education. As new Christians become involved in church, they should be encouraged to take advantage of opportunities to learn and grow in their faith. The *Bible-study program* of a church will help the new member grow in Bible knowledge, as well as improve his skills in using and studying the Bible. Bible-study groups also involve the new member in fellowship with other Christians his age. The *discipleship-training ministry* of a church will help the new member grow in discipleship by learning Christian beliefs, ethics, and ministry skills. Discipleship groups also offer important occasions for Christian fellowship in a caring environment.

> **What help does a baby need from adults to survive? Point out parallels with the kind of help new Christians need for healthy spiritual growth.**

_____

_____

_____

_____

_____

The Profession of Faith

One of the great challenges in personal witnessing is leading someone who accepts the Lord in her home to make a profession of faith at church and to be baptized. One of your responsibilities as a witness is to help new believers understand the significance of baptism and church membership. Three issues are involved in making a profession of faith: public identification, baptism, and church membership.

Public identification. When Jesus called persons to follow Him, He usually did so publicly. He called Matthew at his job (see Matt. 9:9). He called Zacchaeus in front of a crowd on the side of a road (see Luke 19:1-6). In Mark 8:38 Jesus said that He would be ashamed of those who were ashamed of Him before others. Jesus expected persons who followed Him to do so publicly.

Explain to a new convert how to make a public profession

of faith. This can be done even if the person does not join your church. Describe how the invitation system works in your church. Offer to walk forward with him if he would like for you to do so. Invite the convert to church with you the Sunday after he receives Christ. If possible, introduce the person to the pastor before the worship service. You should be willing to stand in the receiving line and make introductions to help the new believer feel at home.

Baptism. To acknowledge Jesus as Lord is to accept the responsibility to obey Him. The Bible clearly teaches that baptism is an expected expression of a commitment to Jesus Christ (see Matt. 28:19; Acts 8:35-38; Rom. 6:4). Although baptism does not save us, it is the visible expression of our inner commitment to Christ as our Savior and Lord.

A Christian's baptism is also important to others. The act of baptism by immersion portrays what Jesus did for us. He died for our sin and was resurrected from the grave for our new life. Going under the water represents death, and coming up from the water represents new life. Baptism is a picture or an illustration of our salvation. Our sin has been buried and put away. We have new life in Jesus. When we are baptized, we are showing others what Jesus did for us. It is a form of witnessing.

When you talk to a new Christian about baptism, focus on the issues of obedience and witness. Help the person look at what Scripture says about baptism. If the person is not ready to be baptized immediately, be patient but persistent. Baptism really is important.

Fill in the blanks.

When I knew that I needed to make a profession of faith,

I felt _____.

Walking down the aisle during the invitation was a
_____ experience for me.

One thing I can do to encourage someone to make a
profession of faith is _____.

Church membership. One who professes faith in Jesus
Christ and is baptized should be an active member of a local
church. Hebrews 10:24-25 emphasizes the importance of
gathering together as the body of Christ: "Let us consider
how we may spur one another on toward love and good
deeds. Let us not give up meeting together, as some are in
the habit of doing, but let us encourage one another—and
all the more as you see the Day approaching." At church
Christians receive nurture and encouragement. It is also the
place where believers are to be equipped for ministry.

As a baby could not survive without a home and a family,
a new Christian will have a difficult time developing a
healthy relationship with God apart from fellowship with
other believers. God intended spiritual babies to find help
and encouragement in the family of faith, the church. New
Christians may think of the church as a building. Help them
understand that it is also a gathering of persons who love
and serve Jesus together. Church membership and
participation also illustrate our submission to the lordship
of Christ.

Witness for Christ

Many new Christians will have more unsaved friends at the
time of their conversion than at any other time in their lives.
Witnessing is a job not just for the spiritual elite of the
church. It is the responsibility of each person who has been

saved. Converts should learn from the beginning their opportunity and obligation to tell others about the Lord.

Challenging new Christians to witness involves little more than channeling the natural impulse we all have to tell others what happens in our lives. When genuine conversion takes place, a person will want to tell the persons he knows best about what happened. Your job is to identify that desire as the initial fulfillment of a lifelong responsibility to tell others about Jesus. What we want to share with friends and family members Jesus wants us to share at every opportunity for the rest of our lives.

Ask the new Christian to identify one person who would be interested to know about his conversion. Have him identify another person who needs what Jesus can do. Let the convert suggest a time when he can tell each one about his salvation experience. If he designates a definite time, he will be more likely to follow through. Explain that telling others what Jesus has done for us is called witnessing and that Jesus has assigned every Christian that job. Use Matthew 4:19 and 2 Corinthians 5:18,20 as scriptural references. Volunteer to go with him if he would like some help in explaining what happened to him.

The best evangelistic prospects that a person will ever have are the ones he knows at the time of his conversion. If you help new Christians learn to witness, every profession of faith can lead to others.

The work of the witness is not finished when someone accepts Christ. As witnesses we are responsible to help the new Christian become a growing, active disciple of Jesus. The burning desire of Paul the apostle should be ours, as well: "We proclaim him, admonishing and teaching everyone with all wisdom, so that we may present everyone perfect in Christ. To this end I labor, struggling with all his energy, which so powerfully works in me" (Col. 1:28-29).

Who are some of the persons new Christians would want to tell about their conversion?

_____

_____

_____

How would you suggest that a new Christian approach telling a family member or a friend about becoming a Christian?

_____

_____

_____

You have finished your training. How do you plan to use it to tell others about Jesus?

SHARE THE GOOD NEWS
Share as the Lord leads you this week.
If you have led someone to the Lord during this study, write down what you need to do to encourage him in the areas considered in this chapter. Then follow through with your plan.

---

[1]WRITE LifeWay Church Resources Customer Service; One LifeWay Plaza; Nashville, TN 37234-0113; FAX order to (615) 251-5933; PHONE (800) 458-2772; EMAIL to *customerservice@lifeway.com*; ORDER ONLINE at *www.lifeway.com;* or VISIT the LifeWay Christian Store serving you.
[2]Survival Kit is available from LifeWay Church Resources Customer Service.

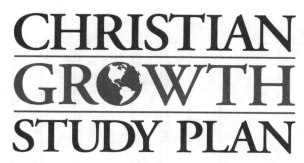

CHRISTIAN GROWTH STUDY PLAN

Preparing Christians to Serve

In the **Christian Growth Study Plan (formerly Church Study Course),** this book *Learning to Share My Faith: A Practical Guide for Successful Witnessing* is a resource for course credit in the subject area Evangelism of the Christian Growth category of plans. To receive credit, read the book, complete the learning activities, show your work to your pastor, a staff member or church leader, then complete the following information. This page may be duplicated. Send the completed page to:

Christian Growth Study Plan
One LifeWay Plaza
Nashville, TN 37234-0117
FAX: (615)251-5067
Email: *cgspnet@lifeway.com*

For information about the Christian Growth Study Plan, refer to the Christian Growth Study Plan Catalog. It is located online at www.lifeway.com/cgsp. If you do not have access to the Internet, contact the Christian Growth Study Plan office (1.800.968.5519) for the specific plan you need for your ministry.

Learning to Share My Faith
Course Number CG-0077

PARTICIPANT INFORMATION

Social Security Number (USA ONLY-optional)	Personal CGSP Number*			

Name (First, Middle, Last)		Home Phone	Date of Birth (MONTH, DAY, YEAR)

Address (Street, Route, or P.O. Box)	City, State, or Province	Zip/Postal Code

CHURCH INFORMATION

Church Name		

Address (Street, Route, or P.O. Box)	City, State, or Province	Zip/Postal Code

CHANGE REQUEST ONLY

☐ Former Name	City, State, or Province	Zip/Postal Code
☐ Former Address	City, State, or Province	Zip/Postal Code
☐ Former Church	City, State, or Province	Zip/Postal Code

Signature of Pastor, Conference Leader, or Other Church Leader	Date

*New participants are requested but not required to give SS# and date of birth. Existing participants, please give CGSP# when using SS# for the first time. Thereafter, only one ID# is required. **Mail to:** Christian Growth Study Plan, One LifeWay Plaza, Nashville, TN 37234-0117. Fax: (615)251-5067.

Rev. 5-02